DIGITAL AND INFORMATION LITERACY

INTERNET
SURVEILLANCE
AND HOW TO
PROTECT YOUR PRIVACY

KATHY FURGANG

rosen publishing's
rosen central®

New York

Published in 2017 by The Rosen Publishing Group, Inc.
29 East 21st Street, New York, NY 10010

Library of Congress Cataloging-in-Publication Data

Names: Furgang, Kathy, author.
Title: Internet surveillance and how to protect your privacy / Kathy Furgang.
Description: New York : Rosen Publishing, 2017. | Series: Digital and information literacy | Includes bibliographical references and index.
Identifiers: LCCN 2016018584| ISBN 9781508173205 (library bound) | ISBN 9781499465198 (pbk.) | ISBN 9781499465204 (6-pack)
Subjects: LCSH: Internet—Security measures—Juvenile literature. | Internet—Safety measures—Juvenile literature. | Computer security—Juvenile literature. | Data protection—Juvenile literature. | Consumer protection—Juvenile literature.
Classification: LCC TK5105.875.I57 F87 2017 | DDC 004.67/8—dc23
LC record available at https://lccn.loc.gov/2016018584

Manufactured in China

CONTENTS

INTRODUCTION

When you hear the term "internet surveillance," you might picture people sitting in rooms tracking your every move on the internet. Or you might picture a Hollywood thriller with spies. They would be peeking in your windows with binoculars to see what you are searching on the internet. Don't worry, however. Internet surveillance is nothing like either of these. Instead it is the broad term for the practice of gaining information from online sources. There are many types of internet surveillance. For example, government agencies might monitor suspected criminals online. This is to protect the public from danger. Or, a private company might take note of your online habits and tastes in order to target advertising to you. In both of these cases, the practices are not meant to interrupt, or interfere with, people's lives. They are meant to benefit people. This can involve either protecting them from harm or making them aware of goods or services they may want.

It's good to know that internet surveillance is not usually meant to do us harm. That does not mean there are not people who try to do harm on the internet. It's important to keep our private information private. There are people who use the internet to steal valuable, personal information. This includes credit card numbers, Social Security numbers, and other personal data that can be used in crimes.

Internet surveillance exists worldwide, with much of it meant to do no harm at all.

No matter how hard we try, it is almost impossible to keep some of our personal details off the internet. Even if we don't put this information online personally, it may end up there anyway. For example, let's say you shop in a store with a credit card. Chances are your credit card number will be sent over the internet, even if you shop in a store instead of online.

In 2013, in the middle of the busy holiday shopping season, criminals pulled off a huge heist. They stole access to more than forty million credit card numbers from shoppers at the popular retail store Target. The information was taken on its way from the stores to the online databanks were it is stored. This is called an internet breach. Someone interrupted the flow of sensitive information over internet lines. These card numbers could have been sold on the black market. That refers to an illegal trade channel for trafficking goods that are difficult to come by.

Since then, Target has taken many steps to assure that its customers' details are safe in its online systems. However, users can't just rely on large companies to keep their data safe. Everyone must take steps to protect their own privacy and personal information.

In this resource, you will learn important ways that you can protect your privacy on the internet. You'll learn about ways information is shared in today's online world. You'll learn common-sense tips about behaviors that will protect you from online criminals. You'll also learn ways to be tech-savvy to make your computer as safe as possible from attack.

Chapter 1

Who's Watching You on the Internet?

Sometimes it might seem like *everyone* is watching you on the internet. Surveillance comes in many forms. Some of it is to gather information. This could be for protection, data storage, or consumer uses. Other forms of it are meant to cause harm.

It's important to note that there is a big difference between legal internet surveillance and illegal hacking. While some forms of hacking are harmless, other forms are illegal and predatory. The negative kind aims at taking private data without permission. Surveillance done for data collection or crime prevention is legal when done by the right sources. Police and private companies are allowed to collect a certain amount of data from private citizens.

Information Gathering

Some people feel uncomfortable with any form of data collection or surveillance of their personal information. But avoiding the internet is not a reasonable way to address the problem. Even if you choose not to do any business online, your information is still out there.

Databases

Suppose you refuse to do internet banking. You might fear that people are spying on your personal information. You don't want to put your bank accounts or Social Security number online. The bank will still have your details in its online databases. Yes, even if you are not aware of it. Businesses today store most of their data online. That means that your data is online, even if you did not choose to put it there.

Many employers have done away with giving their employees paychecks. Instead, they deposit money directly into employee bank

Even if you don't access bank accounts online, your bank likely keeps customers' sensitive information in online databases.

accounts. When you are older and get a job, chances are the company you work for may store your data in an online database. Human resources departments have a lot of sensitive information about employees. That includes Social Security numbers. They also have information about your retirement accounts and health benefits. Then the company can keep track of changes to your information. They can track you online. Even though you may not have put the details there, it still exists. Your address, phone number, and other personal data are being tracked online.

Consumer Researchers

Your personal internet habits are being watched online, also. Using certain search engines means that you are agreeing to have what you do tracked.

Check the privacy policies of the search engines you normally use. Google has a long privacy statement that describes how it uses your information.

Google, Bing, and Yahoo! search engines all have privacy policies. For instance, if you use Google for services such as email, Google Drive, or Google Chrome, you will have to sign up for an account. Once you sign up, you agree to Google's privacy policy. Many people don't even read these policies. However, you can check them out to see what you have agreed to.

Once you are logged in, go to the Google search engine and click on the word "Privacy" in the lower right-hand side of the screen. The long policy statement states that Google is allowed to collect information about you. That includes your location, the searches you make online, and other details. It can even store credit card numbers you use to make online purchases.

Very often these details are sold to advertisers. They receive large amounts of data about users and their searching habits. Suppose you recently bought, or even just searched for, shoes online. You will then be targeted with ads for shoes when you visit other websites.

This helps advertisers focus their advertising. By such means they can reach an audience that they think will most likely purchase their products. Some people do not mind this targeted advertising. Others feel it is an invasion of their privacy. Chapter 3 explores ways to avoid this type of tracking by corporations.

Government Surveillance

The government also watches people on the internet. In 2013, a secret government program was revealed to the public. It is called PRISM, and it allows for surveillance of internet activity. The USA PATRIOT Act seeks to protect Americans from terrorist activity. This allows for some digital surveillance of the public by the National Security Administration. People were surprised to hear about the large amounts of data collection. However, the government revealed that more than fifty terror plots were avoided due to this effort. Officials were able to use the data to track the activity of

Since the USA PATRIOT Act was passed in October 2001, government officials have defended it and online surveillance as a way to keep Americans safe.

potential terrorists. They then made arrests before the terrorist acts were carried out. One of the plots that was prevented was an attack on the New York City subway system. Who knows what other crimes may be prevented in the future?

Even today, some terrorists who escaped after terror attacks such as the ones in Paris, France or Boston, Massachusetts were already known to the government. This doesn't mean that they can always be caught beforehand. The surveillance allowed officials to track and monitor them. This can help to find the criminals after illegal acts are carried out.

Privacy vs. Public Safety

Consumers can try to protect themselves from privacy breaches. But can their efforts be undone by government agencies? In 2016, the Federal Bureau of Investigation (FBI) made a request of the company Apple. It wanted help gaining access to data on one of Apple's customer's iPhones. This data was protected. The customer whose phone it was happened to be a terrorist. He died in a shooting in San Bernardino, California. The FBI believed the phone could help it with its investigation. But the phone was protected by a passcode that the FBI could not crack. The FBI asked Apple to help it gain access to the phone by bypassing the passcode. This would cause Apple to hack its own product. Apple refused to do so. It felt the action would disrupt all of its phones' security. It would make it easier for the FBI to demand that it undo its privacy features in the future. The company has worked hard to ensure the privacy of its users. In the end, the FBI got what it wanted. It used other methods to access the phone's data. However, the question still stands. How much privacy should a consumer really have? Does the government have the right to your personal details?

Dangers

Not all surveillance is for a good intention, such as to stop criminals. Some of it is performed by criminals themselves. This is why protecting your personal information is so important.

Online Predators

Some criminals pose as other people on social media and strike out against others. They might do something as simple as bully another online user on Facebook or Twitter. Or they can commit serious crimes. Online criminals tend to get to know the people they are stalking. They do this in order to gain their trust. After that, a personal meeting might be set up. The person being stalked is likely not aware of the other person's bad intentions.

Hackers

Hackers are people who have a lot of computer knowledge. They can sometimes use it to break into secure systems. They are looking to steal digital information. Hackers commit what law officials call cyber crimes. According to an article by DigitalTrends.com, the computer security company McAfee did a study on cyber crime. It was done along with the Center for Strategic and International Studies. The study found that cyber crimes cost an enormous amount of money around the world. This figure tops $575 billion a year. The United States had the largest amount of cyber crimes with the largest financial losses.

Even a modest estimate puts the amount over $375 billion in a year. Compare that to the cost of some natural disasters. Hurricane Sandy, the 2012 storm that hit the East Coast of the United States, cost $65.7 billion in damages. Now you can see what a problem cyber crime has become. Police are as concerned about it as many of the corporations targeted with the crimes.

Hackers perform massive data breaches. They can steal millions of dollars from consumers and businesses. Those companies could easily be put out of business if they don't protect their customers. For example, suppose a consumer has a credit card hacked online. The thief might charge thousands of dollars on the card. The credit card company would have to pay for that expense. That is not the only effect. The company would also want to protect all of its other customers from the same problem. That

In 2013, the popular retailer Target had an electronic data breach that put the personal information of thousands of customers at risk.

could mean spending millions or billions of dollars to keep data safe. Protecting data could mean developing new software to protect databases. This can be costly for companies. This is because such systems require constant monitoring and updating.

Large data breaches are even more troublesome. Companies that have been breached may lose the trust of their customers. Like the Target breach of 2013, thousands of customers are put in harm's way. New credit cards must be issued to all customers. Many of these customers may choose not to shop at the store anymore. Costly advertising campaigns may result. They aim to restore people's trust in the company and its brand. Data breaches of large companies can be dangerous to national security as well. Some of these companies may do business with and for the government. If hackers gain access to this data it could endanger products, missions, or other plans.

Chapter 2

Being Tech Savvy to Protect Privacy

t's true there's no way to avoid having our personal information on the internet. Still, there are steps we can take to secure it. Some common-sense steps can go a long way to make our behavior better online. The tips you will learn in this chapter can help you use the internet responsibly.

Create Smart Passwords

Having a good internet password for a website is like having a good lock on your front door. A password can keep unwanted users from accessing your details. You'll find that many websites are set up carefully. They try to protect your privacy so well that even you can't access it without just the right information.

When hackers steal information, they may do it by guessing weak passwords. Internet company SplashData makes an annual "Worst Passwords List." It shows some of the weakest and most common passwords that people use. The top three weakest passwords of 2015 were, "123456,"

A good password can do a lot to keep your personal information safe. Choose your passwords wisely.

"password," and "12345678." Others include "football," "baseball," "111111," and "abc123." What's more, most of these passwords have been on the list for years. That means that most people have not even made an effort to be safer online.

The safest passwords have both letters and numbers. They often have capital letters and symbols, too. Some websites won't even let people use passwords that don't have both numbers and letters. A password with both letters and numbers is called alphanumeric.

It's smart to also try a password that others can't guess. For example, choose a quote from your favorite movie or book. Then make the first letter of each word in the quote a part of your password. For instance, consider the quote "And They Lived Happily Ever After." It can turn into a password using the first letter of each word, or "ATLHEA." Try making every other letter capital, such as, "AtLhEA." To include a number, add one in the beginning or end. Or you can replace words like "for" with "4" or "one" with "1." Replacing other letters with symbols can help, too. Replace an "S" with "$." Replace "a" with "@." Each symbol or number you add makes the password harder for a hacker to guess.

Once you have made passwords, be sure to write them down. It may be easy to remember the quote from your favorite movie or book. But it might be hard to remember how you adjusted the quote with special symbols or capital letters.

In addition to making alphanumeric passwords, change your passwords often. Sometimes data breaches are not revealed to the public until months later. If someone keeps up on changing his or her passwords frequently, they will be less likely to be guessed or cracked.

Use Different Passwords

The older you get, the more internet accounts you will have. It's smart to keep different passwords for different accounts. This is especially true if the sites deal with your money. Keep the passwords for banking information different from ones for credit cards. If a hacker is able to get one password, that person may be able to quickly gain access to multiple accounts if the password is the same on each site.

Keep a list of your multiple passwords and what they are for. To be totally secure, keep the usernames for the sites in a different location. If you use the sites often or can stay logged in on your computer, you won't need to refer to the list often. But it's important to have easy access to it. Update the list each time you update a password.

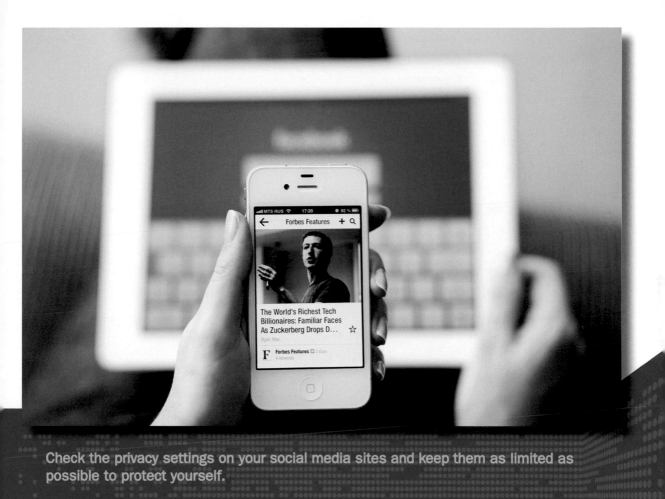

Check the privacy settings on your social media sites and keep them as limited as possible to protect yourself.

Set Internet Privacy Settings

Think about all of the social media websites you visit. Each one of them has privacy settings that you can control. Each one of your Facebook or Instagram posts, for instance, can be sent to people you have approved as friends or followers. Or, you can have your account set so that everyone can see or access your posts, even strangers. This can be dangerous in a world of online predators.

19

It's best to set your social media privacy settings as strictly as possible. Allowing strangers a view into your online life is a good way to open yourself up to predators. If you were in a public place, you wouldn't show strangers pictures of what you and your friends are up to. It makes sense not to do it online, either.

Remember that computer settings for a social media site are different than the ones on your mobile app for the same site. Be sure to set the privacy settings in each location to ensure that your information is secure.

Stay Private

Our general behavior on the internet can help protect us. The way we talk on social media can reveal a lot of personal details about us, like where

The mask shown here has become a symbol of the worldwide hacktivist group known as Anonymous.

we are, who we are with, and what we are doing. Being cautious of what we reveal about ourselves can protect us and our friends and family. Even people you think you know could pose a threat. Consider how well you know a person before you accept him or her as a follower.

Private information should also be kept private in emails. Some hackers use scams to get personal information out of people. These scams are called phishing. They can include fake emails designed to imitate emails from financial institutions. They might ask you to click on a link and then enter your account details. Keep in mind that real financial institutions will not call or email you to ask for this information. Be very cautious of data you give out online. Make sure a trusted adult is present before you do any interactions or communication on the internet.

File   Edit   View   Favorites   Tools   Help

ANONYMOUS

Anonymous

Is there such a thing as a "good" hacker? An unofficial, international group of hackers says so. They are known as Anonymous. They take part in hacking around the world. Their activities are just as illegal as the hacking done by thieves on the internet. But the group hacks entertainment companies and even governments as a form of activism. In other words, they do it to protest actions or laws that they feel are unfair. These "hactivists" remain completely anonymous. They appear in public or in the media wearing stylized masks of the historical figure Guy Fawkes. He is famous for planning a plot against the British government in the early 1600s.

Be Cautious on Public Wi-Fi

When you bring your laptop to a local café or sign up to use public Wi-Fi with your smartphone, you may be using unprotected networks. That means that everyone is working off the same internet connection. If you don't have all of the privacy settings on your computer set correctly, a hacker can gain access to your computer without a password. Don't enter passwords on public Wi-Fi. If someone is monitoring the work being done there, he or she can gain access to your computer. Chapter 3 will discuss how to protect your online privacy.

Remember that most public Wi-Fi is unprotected, which can put your personal information at risk when you surf the internet.

Keep in mind also that some public Wi-Fi spots are fake. A hacker can create a fake public Wi-Fi spot named for a local café or location. When people log on, they think it belongs to the café. Then the hacker gets people's information. He can even see all of your keystrokes. This means he can steal any personal information that you enter. If you are unsure about which Wi-Fi connection belongs to the public place you are in, be sure to ask someone the name of the Wi-Fi network so you choose the correct one.

TEN GREAT QUESTIONS

TO ASK AN INTERNET SECURITY SPECIALIST

1 How often should I check my privacy settings on websites that I use frequently?

2 I keep a list of all of my separate passwords. But what can I do to keep my passwords safe?

3 Is there a way to tell if my computer has been hacked?

4 Does antivirus software really work to protect my computer against viruses?

5 What should I do if I suspect my computer privacy has been breached?

6 Am I more likely to put my computer at risk if I go to some websites than others?

7 Should I ever be giving my computer passwords to tech-support technicians when I call for computer help?

8 If the Wi-Fi in a public place requires a password to access it, can I consider it safe?

9 Should I be worried about my privacy and computer security when lending my computer to a friend?

10 How can I learn more about internet security?

Chapter 3

Getting Tech Help

ommon-sense methods are necessary to keep your information safe from online predators. There are also steps you can take to make your computer safer. Although every model and make of computer is different, each one has privacy settings. You should make yourself familiar with these settings before searching online or working in a public setting with a laptop. Follow any security instructions that come with

When you first set up your computer, set all internet security settings to provide the most protection possible.

your computer, and follow them carefully. Any internet browser you choose should be set to its fullest security settings as well. Have an adult help you set up these systems when you first receive your computer.

Setting up the security features of your computer includes an important step. Make sure any file-sharing features are turned off between your computer and any other computer on the network that you share. File-sharing can be very convenient in a home or small business setting in which the users need to share files. But if you leave this feature on when at an internet café, your files may be at risk if someone is watching the public network. If you do not have a reason for sharing files at home, leave the file-sharing feature off. You don't want to forget about it accidentally.

Antivirus Software

One of the most common ways people keep their computers safe from harm is by installing antivirus software. Many people do this when they first get the computer. PC computers, as opposed to Macs, can be more prone to getting computer viruses. Virus programs are so vital, in fact, that they are often sold along with the computer. Your computer may also warn you to install such software as the computer starts up. Have an adult help you set this up.

Prevent Spyware and Adware

Spyware and adware are types of malware, or harmful computer software. Spyware is software that allows someone to obtain information about another computer secretly by taking it from the hard drive. Spyware can track the keystrokes you make. This reveals passwords and other personal or valuable information.

Spyware can also change your computer settings. This may make your computer work very slowly or redirect your searches. It can even keep you from connecting to a network entirely.

Making your computer secure from malware and other intrusions into your privacy is like locking it up for safety.

Most people get spyware attached to their computers by downloading software that they wanted for their computer. The spyware will enter the computer through the installation process. It begins infecting the computer at once. Sometimes the malware is even attached while people install security software meant to *protect* the computer. While PC computers are more likely to be infected with spyware than Mac computers, all types of computers have been known to be infected.

Make sure you only download software from a trusted site, such as the website of the company that makes the software. Before you download, read any user agreements to look for language about information gathering. Also, be especially careful about downloads for antispyware programs. These programs might ask you to click on a button to start a scan for spyware. Next they might tell you to download a product to fix the spyware they find on your computer. That ends up infecting it. Use only antispyware programs from legitimate companies. One way to do this is to buy them in a computer store instead of online.

Adware display ads use pop-up windows. These may track your advertising settings in order to focus advertising directly at you. Adware is not usually harmful. Still, many consider it an invasion of privacy. Removing it or preventing it along with spyware is a common practice. It helps to make your computer as safe and streamlined as possible.

File   Edit   View   Favorites   Tools   Help

IDENTITY THEFT

Identity Theft

What can someone do with the information gained from malware? One of the most popular uses is identity theft. Identity thieves use the information they find to pose as another person. This includes credit card information along with security questions. It also includes phone numbers, addresses, and Social Security numbers. All of the things are asked for by customer service representatives when you complete telephone or online transactions. Identity theft victims may have a difficult time proving they have been cheated and did not make the transaction. The more people do online, the more important it is to take precautions against identity theft.

Keep Trackers Away

In the previous chapter, you learned that major internet search engines sell information about their users to advertisers. They may also make your details known to government agencies. Keep in mind that this is only possible when you are logged in to your account. For example, staying logged in to your Gmail account with Google or being logged in to Google Drive makes your internet searches trackable. If you really want to stay private, log off of these accounts before searching. You can also do your searches on another web browser that is not logged in to an account that has collected your data. This will help keep your searches private.

Firewall

A firewall is a part of a computer network or computer system. It is meant to block unauthorized access into the computer. At the same time, it allows you to communicate outside of the system, such as on the internet. A firewall can be hardware-based or software-based. Some come already installed with the computer. As you purchase your computer, ask about this feature. This helps to make sure that you are protected as you connect to a network.

Third-Party Cookies

A third-party cookie is data saved by your web browser about websites you have visited. It is meant as a way for a website to track your preferences. It also makes it easier for you to find places you have visited. This can be a privacy concern for many users, however, because it provides a history of their searching habits and website visits. These third-party cookies can be blocked and cleared. Each web browser has a different way of clearing the data, so look it up online and follow the instructions. Most involve going into the web browser preferences to clear and disable the cookies.

Cookies are meant to make finding websites you have visited easier for you. Setting bookmarks for the most important sites should be sufficient for returning to sites that you visit frequently.

File encryption is a more advanced way to protect data from being intercepted and read by other computer users.

Encrypting Program

For someone who wants to prevent all chances of someone intercepting and reading a file that you create on your computer, encryption may be the answer. Encryption is a method of protecting data. Data is converted to a code that makes it unreadable to others. Encryption software can be used to code anything you want. This can mean just one or two personal files, all emails, or everything you create. There are many encryption software packages available. Be sure to get one from a reputable company. Read reviews about it before installing it on your computer. It's also important to read the instructions fully before installing any program, including an encryption program.

Once an encryption program is installed and a file is encrypted, the person receiving the file must also be able to read the same encryption on his or her end. This means that both the sender and receiver must have the same encryption programs. Each also needs a password to access the information.

MYTHS & FACTS

ABOUT INTERNET SURVEILLANCE

MYTH My Internet carrier is spying on me for the government.

FACT In order to carry out its data collection programs, the US government organization called the National Security Agency (NSA) does receive regular deliveries of data from internet and phone carriers. However, the information is not previewed first by your internet carrier, and all users are treated in the same way.

MYTH The government is reading all of my emails.

FACT The NSA collects information about phone calls and internet activity of Americans and people from other countries communicating with Americans. However, the information is not used unless illegal activity is suspected. The sheer volume of information is too much for the government to go through otherwise. These allowances are put in place as part of the USA PATRIOT Act. It is legislation meant to protect Americans from terrorist activities.

MYTH Getting a computer virus will damage my computer's hardware.

FACT When computer viruses infect a computer, it's the software that becomes damaged, not the hardware. While your computer is definitely being damaged when it is infected by a virus, the physical hardware will be unaffected. If the software problems can be removed successfully, your computer will still be usable.

Chapter 4

Keep Up to Date

What happens once you've learned everything there is to know about internet surveillance and how to protect yourself? You might think you're done learning. The fact is that you've just gotten started. Technology changes so quickly that new methods to keep up with hackers are always being developed. New computer operating systems are being designed. And hackers are working hard to figure out how to break into them. Staying on top of the latest in computer security is an important part of your online learning. It helps to read frequently about how to stay safe and keep up on what you can do to protect yourself.

One important way to keep up to date on internet security is to follow the news. Every now and again a large data breach occurs, such as at a department store or an online store. The media is notified and suddenly everyone knows about it. If you visited or shopped in the store being reported about, you should check your accounts right away. Take advantage of any monitoring programs the company might offer in response to the breach. Sometimes stolen data might not be used for months after the

Following the news is a good way to keep informed about large internet security breaches that might affect you.

crime. Be sure to keep an eye on your personal information for a long time after the breach.

Keeping up on the news will also inform you about important viruses that have affected many computers. In addition, the news may keep you informed about changes to social media policies that may affect the way your personal information is shared.

Security in Social Media

If you've ever been on social media, you've noticed the often complex policies about how your information is shared. Those rules never seem to last for more than a year or so. Then new policies take their place. It can be difficult to keep up with these changes, which might put your information at risk. For example, if you do not realize that starting on a certain date Facebook will make your connections or birth date accessible to advertisers then you will not have the chance to change any settings that might protect yourself.

Regularly check the privacy notices of social media sites. It may become harder and harder to make an Instagram feed private. Or there

Be wary of people you meet on online dating sites. Don't give too much personal information until you trust the other person.

may be fewer choices about who can view a new Facebook post. Remember that social media provides a look into your personal world. Someone who is savvy, or dishonest, enough could use your photos, check-ins, or status updates to track you.

Also keep up on media reports about ways that online predators lure people in. This can help make you an informed internet user. For example, internet surveillance comes in many forms. From online dating sites to selling websites, predators keep an eye out for users who do not have their guard up. Meeting an online date can be dangerous. Always meet in a public place. If you are selling an item online and can't ship it, try meeting the

File   Edit   View   Favorites   Tools   Help

INTERNET SECURITY AS A CAREER

Internet Security as a Career

If the topic of internet security interests you, then a career in this field may be for you. Internet security specialists often work for companies, making sure the computers and networks are safe from attack. This may involve installing virus software and updating it. Internet browsers may need to be installed, updated, and set up properly. Setting up and maintaining firewalls and monitoring systems are other duties. Most security specialists have a bachelor's degree in computer science or management information systems. Specialists may spend up to five years getting related experience in the field. Then they will usually be qualified to handle the job of internet security specialist. The median pay for these specialists is higher than the national average. Some take certification and training courses and continue their education even after they are working. As with anyone trying to maintain internet security, continual updates and education are important.

person in a public place. Try to avoid giving out your home address. Similarly, if you give your home address for shipping goods, make sure it is through a reputable website that also knows about your transaction.

Keep Up on Government Laws

While there is not much you can do to prevent government data collection, it certainly can help to stay up to date on policies. Know your rights as a citizen. It's hard to claim that your rights are being violated if you do not know what they are. Stay up on media coverage of changes to the USA PATRIOT Act or policy changes at the NSA. This can help you understand what type of data is being collected from all Americans and how it is being used.

So many consumers pay for online purchases with credit cards that companies must always improve protections to keep them safe.

Credit Card Safety

One way to keep hackers away from your data online is to make sure you are using the most up-to-date systems for paying with credit cards. Currently, chip technologies encrypt the data as it is being sent to its location. This can prevent fraud such as the large credit card breaches that have occurred in the past. Newer, safer methods of paying may soon take its place.

For example, some credit card companies are trying to eliminate passwords to access online accounts or pay for items with a debit card. This data can be stolen too easily by people watching accounts. With some credit cards, a new option may be to use a selfie or a fingerprint to identify yourself when you use your card. After downloading an app, some major credit cards allow users to use the selfie to provide authentication when using the card. Other methods may be developed in the future. These include scans of your iris or your heartbeat, or voice identification. Keeping up on new advances can help you keep your details as safe as possible.

Computer Updates

You may get sick of seeing computer updates on your machine. It is important to install them as soon as possible, though. Out-of-date software is more open to attacks. This is because new software updates include ways to prevent hacking.

It's not only the software that needs updating. Also make sure your computer itself is not too old to be compatible with the latest protections. After a few years, computer companies no longer support older operating systems. That means the virus protection and security settings are dangerously outdated. Keep up on your computer hardware and software to make sure you are keeping your data away from risks.

alphanumeric Consisting of both numbers and letters, often useful for password setups.

Anonymous Unofficial group that anonymously performs civil disobedience through hacking of agencies to make a position known.

cookie A small text file made by a website that is stored in a user's computer and is used to track the user's preferences.

data breach An incident in which sensitive or protected information is viewed or stolen by an unauthorized party.

encryption The process of coding a digital file so that it can only be read by someone with a password to decrypt it.

file sharing The ability to transmit files from one computer to another over a network or over the internet.

firewall A part of a computer system that blocks unauthorized access but allows outgoing communication.

hacker A person who gains unauthorized information from computers.

hardware The machinery and physical component of a computer.

identity theft The illegal acquisition of a person's private information needed for proof of identity.

malware Software that is designed to damage, disable, or harm a computer system.

National Security Agency (NSA) Official US organization dedicated to cryptography, or the writing and solving of codes.

software The programs or operating information used by a computer.

spyware Software that allows users to secretly obtain information from another computer.

surveillance Close observation, often in a covert or secret way.

virus Malware that copies itself onto another computer and infects it, causing harm.

Wi-Fi Wireless networking technology that provides high-speed access to the internet or computer networks.

FOR MORE INFORMATION

American Civil Liberties Union
125 Broad Street, 18th Floor
New York, NY 10004
(212) 549-2500
Website: https://www.aclu.org
The ACLU is an organization meant to defend and preserve the rights of US
    citizens as guaranteed in the Constitution.

Canadian Civil Liberties Association
90 Eglinton Avenue E, Suite 900
Toronto, ON M4P 1A6
Canada
(416) 861-1291
Website: https://ccla.org
The CCLU is an organization meant to defend and preserve the rights of
    Canadian citizens as guaranteed in the Constitution.

Center for Democracy and Technology
1401 K Street NW, Floor 2
Washington, DC 20005
(202) 637-9800
Website: https://cdt.org
The CDT is a nonprofit organization dedicated to preserving the security and
    privacy of internets users. It advocates for strong legal controls on
    government surveillance.

Cyber Privacy Project
1 Federal Street
Boston, MA 02110

(617) 951-8000
Website: http://www.cyberprivacyproject.org
The CPP is an organization that researches issues of cyber privacy and
    educates the public about issues related to cyber privacy.

National Security Agency (NSA)
NSA/CSS
Fort Meade, MD 20755-6248
(301) 688-6524
Website: https://www.nsa.gov
The NSA is the US government agency that collects, processes, and analyzes
    intelligence information for the means of national safety and security.

Online Trust Alliance
P.O. Box 803
Bellevue, WA 98008
(425) 455-7400
Website: https://www.otalliance.org
The OTA is a nonprofit organization that helps educate about security and
    privacy on the internet.

Privacy and Access Council of Canada
Suite 330, Unit 440
10816 Macleod Trail
Calgary AB T2J 5N8
Canada
(877) 746-7222
Website: https://pacc-ccap.ca
PACC is a nonprofit organization dedicated to promoting protection of
    privacy and access to information on the Internet.

FOR FURTHER READING

Barchi, Bill. *Child Online Safety Secrets!* Seattle, WA: Amazon Digital Services, 2012.

Coppola, Craig. *25 Tips for Family Internet Safety*. Seattle, WA: Sharp Mind Publishing, 2012.

Culey, Robert. *Issues In Cyberspace: From Privacy to Piracy*. New York, NY: Britannica Educational Publishing, 2011.

Fine, Lawrence G. *Surviving the Internet: A Guide for Parents and Kids*. Seattle, WA: CreateSpace Independent Publishers, 2010.

Grahams, David. *Ultimate Internet Safety: How to Protect Yourself, Your Family, and Your Computer Whilst Using the Internet*. Seattle, WA: Amazon Digital Services, 2015.

Haley, Bryan. *Internet Safety, a Beginner's Guide*. Seattle, WA: Amazon Digital Services, 2013.

Harmon, Daniel. *Careers in Internet Security*. New York, NY: Rosen Publishing, 2011.

McCarthy, Linda. *Digital Drama: Staying Safe While Being Social Online*. Seattle, WA: 100 Page Press, 2013.

Mooney, Carla. *Online Predators*. San Diego, CA: Reference Point Press, Incorporated, 2011.

Ormsby, Richard. *Social Media Survival Guide: How to Protect Your Family's Security Online*. Seattle, WA: Amazon Digital Services, 2015.

Plotkin, Robert. *Privacy, Security, and Cyberspace* (Computers, Internet, and Society). New York, NY: Facts On File, 2011.

Rauf, Don. *Powering Up a Career in Internet Security*. New York, NY: Rosen Publishing, 2015.

Sommers, Michael. *The Dangers of Online Predators*. New York, NY: Rosen Publishing, 2008.

Yearling, Tricia. *How Do I Stay Safe from Online Predators?* Berkeley Heights, NJ: Enslow Publishers, Inc., 2015.

Websites

Because of the changing nature of internet links, Rosen Publishing has developed an online list of websites related to the subject of this book. This site is updated regularly. Please use this link to access this list:

http://www.rosenlinks.com/DIL/Surv

BIBLIOGRAPHY

Carpentier, Megan. "What Your Search History Says About You (And How to Shut It Up)." Huffington Post, October 31, 2013. http://www.huffingtonpost.com/megan-carpentier/what-your-search-history-_b_4179728.html.

Childress, Sarah. "Just the 'Facts': What We Know About the NSA Spying on Americans. *Frontline*, August 26, 2013. http://www.pbs.org/wgbh/frontline/article/just-the-facts-what-we-know-about-the-nsa-spying-on-americans.

Dezenhall, Eric. "A Look Back at the Target Breach." Huffington Post, April 6, 2015. http://www.huffingtonpost.com/eric-dezenhall/a-look-back-at-the-target_b_7000816.html.

Gallagher, Ryan. "From Paris to Boston, Terrorists Were Already Known to Authorities." The Intercept, November 18, 2015. https://theintercept.com/2015/11/18/terrorists-were-already-known-to-authorities.

Geeksquad. "How to Protect Against Spyware." Retrieved April 11, 2016. http://www.geeksquad.com/do-it-yourself/tech-tip/how-to-protect-against-spyware.aspx.

Gilbert, Ben. "What Is Anonymous and What Does It Do?" Tech Insider, November 17, 2015. http://www.techinsider.io/what-is-anonymous-2015-11.

Hightower, Jim. "8 Terrifying Facts About NSA Surveillance." Alternet.org, April 16, 2014. http://www.alternet.org/8-terrifying-facts-about-nsa-surveillance.

Krawczyk, Konrad. "Cyber Crime Costs the World More Money Than Some Natural Disasters Do." Digital Trends, June 10, 2014. http://www.digitaltrends.com/computing/new-study-says-cyber-crime-costs-hundreds-of-billions-per-year.

Lee, Timothy B. "Here's Everything We Know About PRISM to Date." Washington Post, June 12, 2013. https://www.washingtonpost.com/

news/wonk/wp/2013/06/12/heres-everything-we-know
-about-prism-to-date.

Norton. "Catch Spyware Before It Snags You." Retrieved April 11, 2016.
http://us.norton.com/catch-spyware-before/article.

Parkinson, John R. "NSA: 'Over 50' Terror Plots Foiled by Data Dragnets."
ABC News, June 18, 2013. http://abcnews.go.com/Politics/nsa
-director-50-potential-terrorist-attacks-thwarted-controversial/
story?id=19428148.

PC Tools. "What Is Spyware and What does It Do?" Retrieved April 11, 2016.
http://www.pctools.com/security-news/what-is-spyware.

Santana, Marco. "Encrypted Chips Help Fight Credit Card Fraud." *USA
Today*, January 9, 2014. http://www.usatoday.com/story/news/
nation/2014/01/09/encrypted-chips-help-fight-credit-card-fraud/
4400347.

Study.com. "Salary and Career Info for an Internet Security Specialist."
Retrieved April 11, 2016. http://study.com/articles/Salary_and_
Career_Info_for_an_Internet_Security_Specialist.html.

TeamsID. "Worst Passwords of 2015." January 19, 2016. https://www.
teamsid.com/worst-passwords-2015.

Wolff-Mann, Ethan. "Mastercard Wants You to Pay with a Selfie." *Time*,
February 22, 2016. http://time.com/money/4233007/
mastercard-selfie-authentication.

INDEX

About the Author

Kathy Furgang has written dozens of books for young readers, including books for teens about breaking into sports law, getting internships, and choosing a vo-tech track for success in business. She graduated from Fordham University. She lives in upstate New York with her husband and two sons.

Photo Credits

Cover, p. 1 (left to right) Ichumpitaz/Shutterstock.com, Jane Kelly/Shutterstock.com, Brian A Jackson/Shutterstock.com, Maksim Kabakou/Shutterstock.com; p. 5 Dragon Images/Shutterstock.com; p. 8 Georgejmclittle/Shutterstock.com; p. 9 © Anatolii Babii/Alamy Stock Photo; p. 11 Tim Sloan/AFP/Getty Images; p. 14 © iStockphoto.com/Lpettet; p. 17 Georgejmclittle/Shutterstock.com; p. 19 © iStockphoto.com/Erik Khalitov; p. 20 1000 Words/Shutterstock.com; p. 22 © SFL Travel/Alamy Stock Photo; p. 25 pelfophoto/Shutterstock.com; p. 27 Lisa S./Shutterstock.com; p. 30 jijomathaidesigners/Shutterstock.com; p. 34 hidesy/Shutterstock.com; p. 35 AndreyPopov/iStock/Thinkstock; p. 37 Sfio Cracho/Shutterstock.com; cover and interior pages (pixels) © iStockphoto.com/suprun.

Designer: Nicole Russo; Editor: Xina M. Uhl; Photo Researcher: Xina M. Uhl